TIFFANY'S
TABLE
MANNERS
for
TEEN-AGERS

TIFFANY'S TABLE MANNERS *for* TEEN-AGERS

Ives Washburn, Inc.

NEW YORK

ISBN: 0-679-24108-6

Library of Congress Catalogue Card Number: 61-14132

19   20

Text by W. HOVING   Drawings by JOE EULA

MANUFACTURED IN THE UNITED STATES OF AMERICA

Foreword

GOOD MANNERS are as important as good grooming and good behavior. Unfortunately, however, in this day of confused standards, manners are sometimes sadly neglected. This is especially true of table manners.

At Tiffany's our interest in attractive tables set with good china, glass, and silverware makes us equally aware of the importance of good table manners.

But manners must not be stilted, self-conscious, or artificial. Therefore, it is dangerous to have one system, or no system, for home consumption and another for dining out. This is apt to cause dinner-table insecurity later in life.

So, training in table manners must be started early enough to make them automatic. Consequently we submit herewith our version of good table manners. There are other systems, and we don't quarrel with them, but we think this system is attractive, graceful, and above all, natural.

WALTER HOVING

Contents

Let's Be Seated

It is customary for the young man to help the young lady on his right to be seated.

When you both have been seated, *don't* look around like a startled beetle. Turn directly to the young lady on your right and start talking.

First of all, let's get straight which fork or knife to use.

We like the method of placing the flat silver in the order of its use. You take the piece on the outside first.

Some people arrange the silver by size, so you have to learn to tell a fish knife from a meat knife and a fish fork from a meat fork. If there is no fish knife and fork, use the smaller knife and fork for the fish. If you make a mistake, just continue eating. *Don't* put the silver back on the table. Be nonchalant.

The place for the napkin is on the lap. Don't tie it around your neck or stick it in your belt.

The fish or meat will be served to you on your left side. Take the serving fork in your left hand and the serving spoon in your right, holding them as pictured above.

After you have served yourself, place the serving spoon and fork side by side on the platter.

Vegetables should also be placed on your plate. Side dishes, except for salads, are not used at home, only in restaurants.

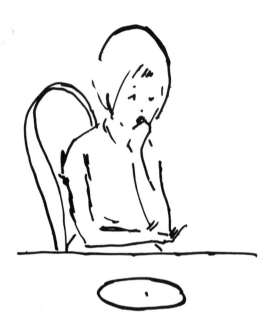

When serving yourself, take small portions. If you don't like what is served, it is permissible to refuse it. But don't find yourself with nothing on your plate. If you do, your hostess may remark about it, which might be embarrassing for you.

You don't have to wait for your hostess to start eating, but don't leap at your food like an Irish wolfhound.

The Soup Course

The soup is brought to the table in the soup plate at dinner.

The soup spoon is held in the right hand with the thumb on top.

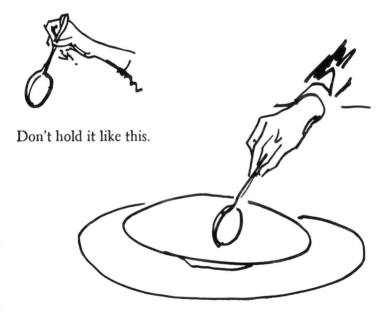

Don't hold it like this.

And don't hold it like a mashie niblick. This is not par for this course.

When you are eating soup, the soup spoon is tipped slightly away from you and is filled by moving it away from you, not toward you. Sip the soup from the side of the spoon or from the end—it makes no difference. And *please*, no noise.

When most of the soup is eaten, tip the soup plate away from you, never toward you. Thus, if you spill some, you will not splash your clothes.

Generally at luncheon soup is served in a cup. This may be eaten with a smaller soup spoon or drunk by lifting the cup.

The Fish Course

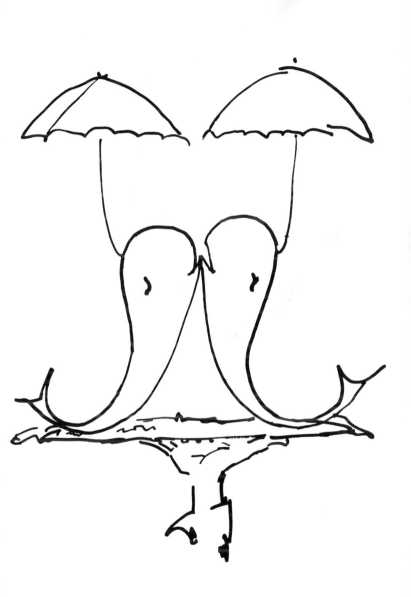

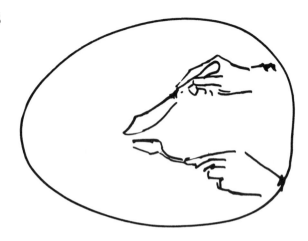

Both the fish knife and fork are used for the fish course.

This is the way to hold the fork. Prongs should *always* be down when the fork is held in the left hand.

This is the way to hold the knife. Note that it differs from the way the meat knife is held.

This is the way to place the fish on the fork. The fork is held in the left hand, and the knife is used to cut and as a pusher.

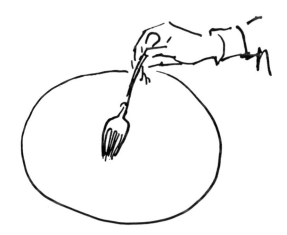

If the fish is soft and boneless, then it is perfectly proper to use only the fish fork. When the fork is held in the right hand, the prongs may be up or down, whichever is more convenient. When you are eating with the fork, don't put the knife on the plate. Leave it on the table. When using only the fork, *never* hold it in the left hand.

The Meat Course

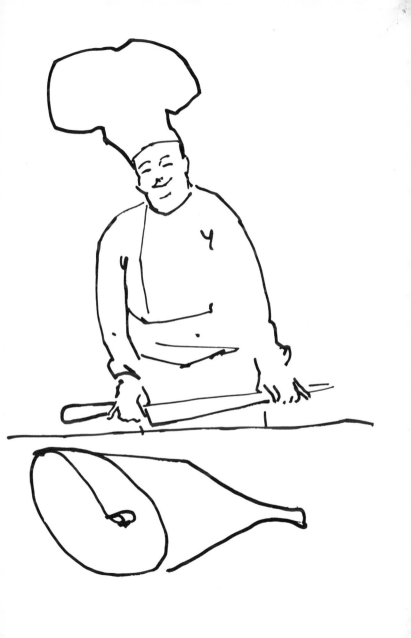

The luncheon or dinner knives and forks are held this way.

The meat knife is not held like the fish knife because more leverage for cutting is necessary. Let the forefinger point down the handle.

And the fork in the left hand. The prongs are always pointed down.

You spear the meat with your fork and cut it off with your knife. Cut only *one* piece at a time. To fix the meat on the prongs of the fork, put the knife blade underneath the piece of meat. A slight twist will help to fix it firmly.

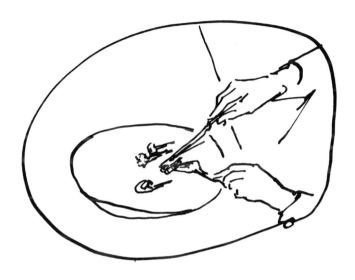

A small amount of potatoes and vegetables may be placed on the prongs of the fork with the meat.

The fork is conveyed to the mouth by twisting your wrist and raising your forearm slightly.

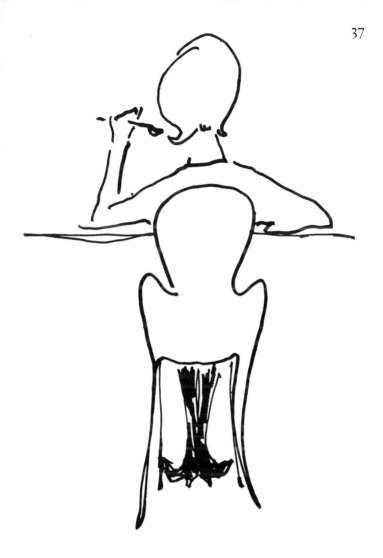

Don't stick your elbow out and raise your whole arm like a derrick.

Each time you take a mouthful, lean over your plate. If anything drops, it will fall on the plate and not on your clothes.

After cutting the meat, never place the knife across the corner of the plate. Don't keep shifting the fork from the left to the right hand. This is clumsy and awkward.

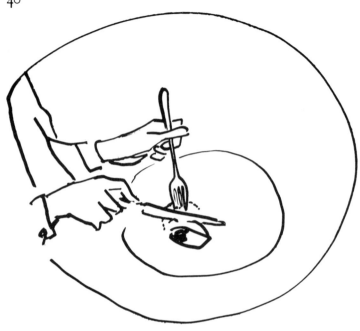

Never hold the fork this way when cutting meat.

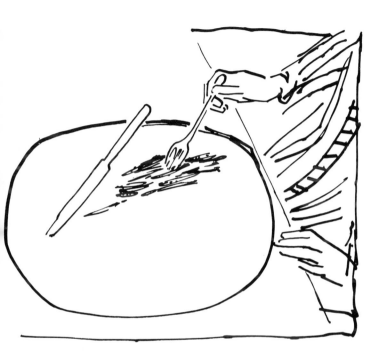

If occasionally you want to eat some vegetables with your right hand, place the knife as above. But do not shift the fork back and forth every time you cut a piece of meat.

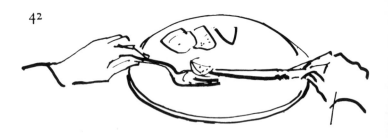

Never hold the fork in the left hand with the prongs up and pile food on it with the knife.

Never hold the knife in the left hand.

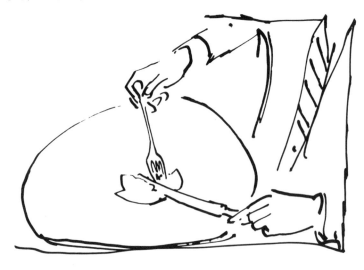

While you are eating, *never* place the knife and fork like a pair of oars in a rowboat.

Always place them like this. This is the *only* "rest" position. The knife and fork are crossed on the plate with the fork over the knife with the prongs pointed down. This is one reason why the prongs are curved. A good butler or waitress will never remove your plate with the knife and fork crossed because he knows that you are not finished.

Never wipe your mouth with one hand while holding a knife or fork in the other.

Never keep the fork in the left hand while drinking
water.

Do not hold the knife and fork in this position when you are talking. It looks unattractive and belligerent.

It is perfectly proper to talk with the knife and fork in your hands but do not gesticulate with the fork or the knife. The knife should *never* be raised more than an inch or two above the plate. If you remember this rule, you'll never get caught with the knife in your mouth.

When eating a piece of bread or drinking, place the knife and fork in the "rest" position. The sharp edge of the knife blade should be pointing to the left. This is the best place for your knife and fork when you are chewing, talking, or wiping your mouth.

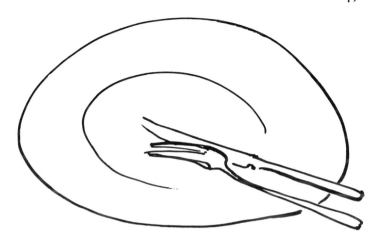

When the course is finished, *always* place your knife and fork as above. The prongs of fork should be down. The blade of the knife should face the fork. This is the "I am finished" position.

If the meat doesn't require cutting with the knife, it may be eaten with the fork in the right hand. In this case don't use the knife at all. Leave it on the table.

When eating only with the fork, place it, *prongs up*, on the plate when you are finished.

The butter knife is placed across the butter plate. Always break the bread with your fingers. Do not cut the bread with the butter knife; just butter the bread with it.

The Salad Course

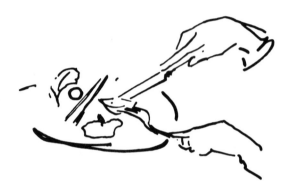

The salad may be eaten with the salad knife and fork just as the fish and meat courses are eaten.

Or if you feel the salad can be cut with the edge of the salad fork, the knife may be left on the table.

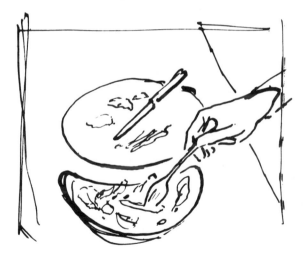

At luncheon, salad is often served at the same time the meat course is served. In this case you may use the same fork you are using for the meat.

Asparagus is eaten with the fingers, unless stalks are too long.

If the asparagus is long and thin, cut off the ends with your fork held in your right hand and eat with your fork. You will then avoid imitating a trained seal. Then pick the shortened stalks up in your fingers.

An artichoke is eaten with the fingers. Pull off the leaves one at a time and draw them through your teeth. Don't try to swallow the whole leaf; it won't digest well.

When you get to the heart, use your knife and fork.

The Dessert Course

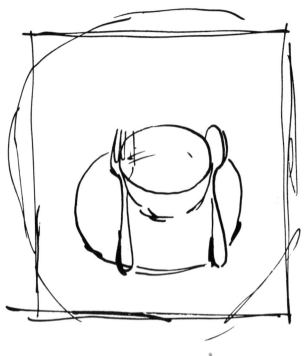

After the meat course the table is cleared of the dinner or luncheon plates and all unused silver. The peppers and salts are also removed, and the table is crumbed.

Then the dessert plate is served as above with the finger bowl, spoon, and fork on the plate.

Remove the finger bowl and place it on the table to the upper left of your plate.

Also remove the fork to the left and the spoon to the right. Do not leave the doily (if any) on your plate by mistake. It is not supposed to be eaten with your ice cream. This would alarm your hostess unduly.

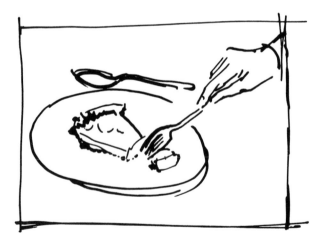

The dessert may be eaten with the fork in the left hand (prongs down) and the spoon in the right. Eat with the spoon. The fork here serves only as a pusher.

If it is pie or cake, only the fork need be used; if ice cream or pudding, the spoon. The other piece is left on the table.

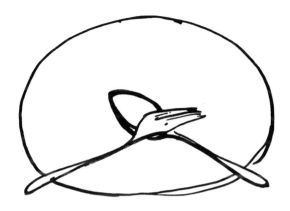

The same "rest" position of the fork and spoon is used as in the case of the knife and fork during the meat course. The fork prongs down, lying over the spoon.

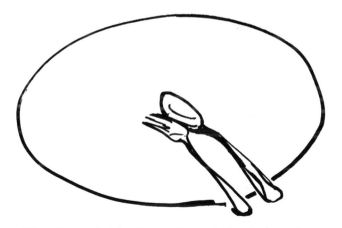

The "I am finished" position of the fork and spoon. Note bowl up, prongs down.

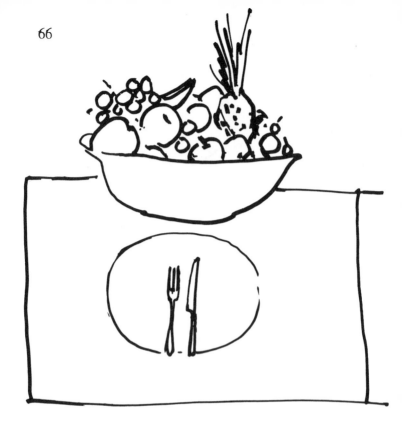

If fresh fruit is served, another dessert or fruit plate is brought in with a fruit knife and fork on it. This is not often done in this country any more, but it is quite common abroad. Take the apple or pear, quarter it with the fruit knife, and peel it. Then eat it, either with the fruit fork or with your fingers. Grapes are eaten with your fingers.

When it comes time to use your finger bowl, dip the tips of your fingers in it. But don't forget, it is not a bath tub; you're not supposed to dunk your whole hand. If you wish, you may also brush the tips of your wet fingers over your mouth. Then wipe your mouth, but don't let the water drip down your chin.

Some Don'ts...

Don't let your elbows stick out like flying buttresses. Keep them close to your sides.

Don't try to eat with your elbows on the table. It hampers your movements, and you may spill your food. Elbows should operate freely. You may, however, rest your elbows on the table when you're not eating.

Don't leave your spoon in your coffee cup.

Don't put too much in your mouth at once. It looks as if you were brought up in a kennel.

Don't chew with your mouth open, and don't smack your lips. Not only is it unappetizing, but it interferes with other people's conversation.

Don't talk with your mouth full. Some of your lunch
might fall out. You must learn, however, to talk with a
little in your mouth, simply because you can't always
wait until you have swallowed everything before answer-
ing a question. So if you take a little at a time, you will
always be ready to join the conversation. This takes skill
and practice.

When eating corn on the cob, hold it in both hands. Don't stick handles into each end as above. It looks too precious and artificial.

Don't eat chicken with your fingers except at a picnic.
With a little practice you can dislodge enough chicken
with your knife and fork to keep body and soul together
till your next meal.

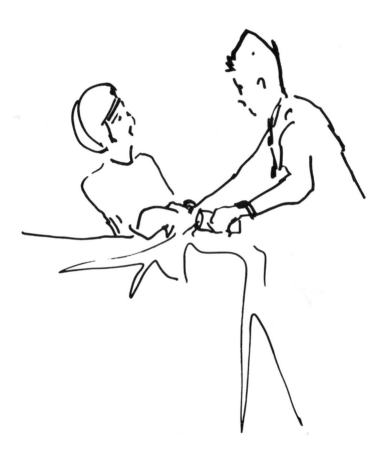

If you knock over your water glass, don't say, "Oops."
Right the glass and keep talking to your partner. *Don't*
start mopping the table with your napkin.

But if you spill the water on your partner's dress, offer her your napkin and say you're sorry. But don't start mopping her. It might be misunderstood.

If you happen to drop your knife or fork on the floor *don't* dive down after it or peer down at it. Pick up another one and proceed according to plan.

Don't try to eat leaning back. It looks awful, and besides you will no doubt spill your food on your shirt.

Sit erect. Don't slouch.

If you find some gristle or a piece of meat you cannot swallow, don't spit it out on your plate or into your fist. Chew it into as small a piece as possible and then place it on the prongs of your fork (or into your spoon if the course calls for a spoon). Then place it on the rim of your plate. Don't let this embarrass you. It is perfectly correct. Olive pits or fish bones should be removed with your fingers.

Don't throw your arm over the back of your chair.

Don't sit on the back of your neck.

Don't air your views in a loud voice.

Be more interested in hearing the other person's views than in expressing your own. That is the essence of good conversation.

When the table "turns," don't get left staring into space. Turn immediately to the girl on your left. If she doesn't turn to you, lean over and say something like this, "How about getting rid of that fascinating fellow on your left and pay a little attention to me?" Don't forget, faint heart never, etc., etc.

If you have to blow your nose don't be embarrassed. Just blow it. But use your *handkerchief*, not your napkin.

If perchance you inadvertently burp or your stomach rumbles, *don't* pat your stomach or your chest, or make any inane remarks about it.

Above all, *be natural. Don't* put on airs or try to be "backstairs refined" by sticking your finger out at a ninety-degree angle when you lift your cup to your mouth. And, *don't* chew your food in a mincing, silly way. Just be yourself.

Don't push a plate away from you when you are through. Leave it where it is with the silverware properly placed.

Don't get up from the table until your hostess rises, and don't leave the dining room until your elders have left it.

So now that you know the rules you can start breaking them. Don't forget, though, it takes a lot of social know-how to break rules.

Remember that a dinner party is not a funeral nor has your hostess invited you because she thinks you are in dire need of food. You're there to be entertaining. Be gay. Do your part. Don't be a gloom.

BON APPETIT!—